first MOUNTAIN

❧

first
MOUNTAIN

∾

PAULETTE DUBÉ

thistledown press

Library and Archives Canada Cataloguing in Publication

Dubé, Paulette, 1963-
First mountain / Paulette Dubé.

Poems.
ISBN 978-1-897235-33-1

I. Title.

PS8557.U2323F47 2007   C811'.54   C2007-904539-1

Cover photograph by Marnie Wilson
Cover and book design by Jackie Forrie
Printed and bound in Canada

Thistledown Press Ltd.
633 Main Street
Saskatoon, Saskatchewan, S7H 0J8
www.thistledownpress.com

Thistledown Press gratefully acknowledges the financial assistance of the Canada Council for the Arts, the Saskatchewan Arts Board, and the Government of Canada through the Book Publishing Industry Development Program for its publishing program.

For Raymond and André

Forget that you are self-important because these mountains don't care about you. They have a long view, in which you are insignificant. They only pay attention to glaciers, and love. Love will always catch them because they don't understand it. So fill up on love if you want to be noticed by mountains.

— Thomas Trofimuk

First day:

this one is quiet
asleep in the basket moon
half way between earth and sky
clear as water singing through my fingers

Second day:

this one born when leaves sing
through first leaf, flex
their sturdy nutmeg arms, wave
fingers flecked with gold

Third day:

safe on the high bank of a bronze green river
loosen this skin with crow feather and sage

the sun rises then

from the Four Directions Gates
come the colours
rattling buffalo skulls behind them
ribbons of children stream
along this day

Fourth day:

cement claw end of a hammer
glare sun squinting eyes, clocks, dead grass, the smell
of carrots, ragged holes, knees, nails, sperm, a sharp
spice of rough hair along my arms, peeling paint
slivers of old steel, dust, rust and rot

Fifth day:

shawl of raven's rose
smells of pale dandelion heart and dirt
there is calm here
no creeping or spilling
as winter's want through cracks
of darkness, this liquid light
simply begins
accepts — rain lays down

a simple miracle

Sixth day:

grandmothers enter the mountains
amid bacon coloured clouds
hang small labradorite pipes on the trees

tobacco ghosts flap yellow red blue white
there is the smell of kerosene

this day will teach us to walk
between anxieties and ego, small rocks
worry your foot when you walk

Seventh day:

there is Moose now
copper taste and smell of sulphur
in her mouth, an agate
in her chest, auroras pulse her veins in all directions

shouldering old bruises aside
she runs
clinging to the backs of mountains

Eighth day:

from under the house comes
a high pitched grunt, wood against metal's sharp

a trench is dug to settle the house
mindful of the proper place for bones

earth things: bones, homes, metal and wood
so too, little piece of flesh from my shoulder
wrapped with tobacco in a fold of red cloth

Ninth day:

here, bottom line
under the eyes
below the ribs
the day unfurls
shimmering as snail trail through the forest

guide and sew silver
or
follow sewn silver

Tenth day:

through a door some see as a fork in the tree
miracles take on the height two eagles can scale
between them, the weight of a shrew's heart
beating as he eats buffalo berries
from a branch no thicker than a feather

Eleventh day:

miracles deliver
precisely the white number of bones in coyote scat
left on the threshold of a door
some see as a fork in the tree

Twelfth day:

rain pulls the sky down
tobacco ties drip in the rain

the moat around our home fills with water
Sparrow takes refuge behind a sheet of plywood
Mouse, between a brick and a large stone
together they scuffle and scratch through birdseed, weeds
rain drums the roof
the hard cracked earth
the backs of birds and mice

my son sleeps
drinking frog medicine in his dreams

Thirteenth day:

promises shape who we are
what we will become, we pray

Fourteenth day:

Mouse under the bird feeder
black eyes sharp and round
taking everything in and storing it for later

if Mouse appears
a duty remains unfulfilled

without the sun
no one works very diligently
best call Owl

Fifteenth day:

our house built on an ancient river bed
is forever, for us, both stone and water
both ship and anchor

Sixteenth day:

Loon fills the space of small hours
as nothing else can

quicken steps to the window
to the edge of the porch
her call wakes me
cell by cell
lit by a liquid throat
tongue of fire

Seventeenth day:

the carpenter we hired tells us
the week of this new moon foretells
stormy weather for a month

there was blood shed
soft hands grew hard
muscles stretched, screamed and dreamed
new shapes as water appeared in all her poses
soft fir planked itself down beneath my feet

my son says it smells like perfume and yes
this month, this battle
this day has breath

Eighteenth day:

Elk bugles across the street
raking, shaking the crab-apple tree
with the tips of his teeth and lips, his immense
rack turns on impossibly thin
legs as Loon sounds from up on the slough, blessing
a new day

Nineteenth day:

smell of smoke from the trees
ever present this season, already tangy in my throat

Muskrat visits today and furs my legs
grown muscular from climbing, bending
stretching over and over again
she insists on playing, hides words in my throat

hold fire with that power
grow trees

Twentieth day:

sweep with a broom of rosemary
sweep, the sun rises
through smoke, Hawk soars overhead

"Hawk is a messenger," I tell my husband
who suckles blood from his torn knuckle
I kiss him and the man next door
comes by to show me the ten stitches he earned for his skull
after a tumble on Indian Ridge

my fingers throb to trace the bruise from his elbow to his broken wrist
to soften the fire in his skull and to help him stop trembling
I give him the broom to hold while I fetch peppermint oil

when I come back, they are both singing a song about home

Twenty-first day:

the sun rises over geraniums in terra cotta pots
Hummingbird darts towards the flowers
that jewelled lady bird
throws back her mossy brass cloak
spirits the cloudless sky

a good home has more windows than walls

Twenty-second day:

white strands of witch hair caught in tree tops
deep in valleys, the sound of running water
running from the sky
running from the earth across rocks
words stream across wind and rain and small red flowers

Twenty-third day:

temper your ambitions
nothing of value was ever created by the sword

Twenty-fourth day:

heat and high cirrus clouds
blazing sun ringed with sun-dogs
water everywhere and nowhere
animals streak the landscape
this one swings gossamer ribbons of colour
north and south
from which direction change comes

Twenty-fifth day:

these sundogs ribbon round
east to west, Squirrel pushes
a large capped mushroom across
the road into the trees, amidst, between
and in spite of dreaming
it is work to survive

when dreams, tall as trees, fly as ash from fires
when fire is reduced to coal memory
we look to mushrooms drying on branches
to feed us when the mean season comes

Twenty-sixth day:

a bone house, supine in tall grass
near the Moberly homestead on the Overlander Trail

take water to the skull, to the mouth
to the space between the eyes
draw circles, hot breath
from the place where sundogs run

sleep the sleep of well earned rest
Elk, life for hunters of land and sky
gift yourself so that others may live
sleep the deep sleep

Twenty-seventh day:

hump of moose hip flayed bent white
neck bones
strewn as stones

        a part

               a ways

skull and jaw tinged pink
a quick red
on the hoof splayed open

wind ruffling what fur's left
a heaped over quilt
soft for a head
small for a bed
splayed split up the middle bone
cracked open and licked clean
only a tuft left

that's how to go
completely used up

Twenty-eighth day:

release crow necklace of small dark tongues to the sky
make way for this day and the light she claims as prize

Twenty-ninth day:

from that dream, astride an elephant
happiness seeped through my seat
this day is grey
wrinkled to withstand the onslaught of family

Thirtieth day:

Owl eating a nectarine
sticks a human tongue from her great grey face
almond eyes unblinking

nothing you do is secret
nothing you think is quiet
you have been weighed
you have been measured
and you have been found wanting

Thirty-first day:

this bend this lend this arm of might
this sap, gold nectar bright

this breath this wind this holy thing
this earth and sky do sing

Thirty-second day:

think on the patient love that cradles man woman egg

in a sand nest made solid under a million year old hand
an egg becomes
dark, oval stone

Thirty-third day:

skim the tops of trees, to get out over water
people gathered there are a little nervous

dreaming, where will I land
they know I can't swim

I fly
like I haven't flown for years

Thirty-fourth day:

this day is born in the wake of geese flying
lance formation threading the air with calls to come
come home
gather yourselves to me
and come home

if yearning were a shape
it would be the lance thrown south
if yearning were sound
it would be geese
and the hot smell of trees burning
rubbing their roots together
anxious to be off

wrapping their shawls of sparkling round
themselves, they turn and wave
wave great arms
wave the smallest finger
turn gracefully on skeletal legs
and melt
to a hard point
on the pale horizon

Thirty-fifth day:

seven stars trace the lessons for women

offer to all directions
small pipe of red earth — breath of life
hold smudge with my lungs

Frog calls Thunder People — echo
calls Thunderbird from the mountains
and again
calling

Thirty-sixth day:

this day is born anxious, wringing hands
cloud temperature pressure stones shifting
water, still on the earth
reflects a face
waits

Thirty-seventh day:

the pileated woodpecker eats from a mountain ash
pyramid of red feathers sits
back on his head flagged by incessant flying
eyes yellow and ancient
fix me, dismiss me

he taps along the trunk, talons curled
weathered and useful
wondering how I manage
to survive, and why

Thirty-eighth day:

mountain cloaked in fog and cold
trail bright with blood bushes
Grouse visits

be still, learn
which battles to take
and which will take you

Thirty-ninth day:

survival embodies existence
but does not define it

Fortieth day:

does grace colour us all the same?
as love's light falls on and over and misses
willow goes before aspen follows birch poplar grasses
all manner of yellow
all softs of brown
wolf willow holds stubborn to dusty green

copper and bronze coins high up in the trees
fall
to pay our weight, our
way through winter

Forty-first day:

the length of the day
is directly proportional to the distance
between you
and the one you love

Forty-second day:

a thorn of experience is worth a wilderness of warning

Forty-third day:

a candle in a church is a thing of beauty, a flame
in the wilderness is a miracle

Forty-fourth day:

pull this from my mouth but do not allow it to shape a sword
stay close, don't let me worry you
see?
the wind blows through me
this hole whistles in the dark, right now in the north

let language lie between us
as tousled sheets in a shared bed
vocabulary of the heart renders us languageless

let me kiss you

Forty-fifth day:

Rabbit, call for me that one
whose absence
a grain of sand, has grown
to the size of all the mountains of this earth

Forty-sixth day:

now that I carry less
I see places of prayer more often

here, a warm space infused with pine and roses
a bull elk lies melting in the sun
eyes closed
head on the ground
snoring

that sound will carry me through the mean season

Forty-seventh day:

a season of sensual repast
rolling between earth and air
dust, grass and leaves
luminescent shades and shape variances
dazzle, intrigue

pay attention to the sharp edge in your life

Forty-eighth day:

there is never enough thank you
for one who feels slighted

Forty-ninth day:

fire and earth
water and air
there is no room for anger there

Fiftieth day:

we need rose geranium, ferocious
violets, coffee and if clouds come
make them twist to grey near the edges, roll them in light
make them forgive you
everything

Fifty-first day:

clear cerulean
this autumn time this
"entre chien et loup" time
this is me
conceived when my parents were happy

Fifty-second day:

a promise chaffs only if
you want to abandon it
otherwise it is another
set of arms
to hold us

Fifty-third day:

children in my dreams
babies that squint
and laugh, I gather to me
feel ghost milk coursing through old dry breast beds

it is good, sustaining milk
and it never ends

Fifty-fourth day:

the last bee flies around me round
and round, seamless
am I, the spinning altar? Am I
the gift?

no less

Fifty-fifth day:

beyond human ears
are whales and elephants
ravens happy in their sky give the same timber
trees travel that tone through bark

this one
this original language
deep in bone
carried in the stomach lining
the hairs on the back of your neck

Fifty-sixth day:

the sound of creek spanking places cool and moss dark
there
the first stone found me
stone shaped like the right foot, foretells a journey to come

a heart of stone
a guardian watches over you

two left feet
journeys made

one swirled with a red sm
life is thus

Fifty-seventh day:

in a torrent of sharp parts leaves
settle on my arms
as brittle and as cold, I blow them to the ground
knowing in a distant way that falling
is the beginning of a journey

Fifty-eighth day:

ahead a little way is Coyote
his fur the colour of tall wheat grass and dry sage
he looks over his shoulder, keeps walking. Stops
when I approach, he lops off the path, to the left.

full moon lights the corners of the universe just fine

Fifty-ninth day:

the wind out there on the laundry line
dances with clothes ghost of my family
waves at the day-moon

I am dancing
les bénédictions de ma famille

Sixtieth day:

hold the first creek ice in your hand
it is enough if you worry about glaciers

smell the ice on your wrist as it melts
it is enough

Sixty-first day:

pick up the penny I have ignored for two days
can't seem to put a foot down
for knocking over a miracle

move the rug back
something this good needs the front door wide open

Sixty-second day:

new moon lives
without casting a shadow
her presence no less palpable

Sixty-third day:

wrap my arms around the tree
breathe into his rough skin
I bleed into leather tethers
break stones
wrist skin torn open

torn open

slow your heart
trust your heart
change the mirror

Sixty-fourth day:

thin sky feeds
blanket of lamb's wool
through narrow soul
such a cold place
a hard place, but
he said
remember
he said *change the mirror*

Sixty-fifth day:

small brown elephant of stone
has only ever three legs on the ground
the fourth lifts in joy

this elephant dances
today that makes all the difference

Sixty-sixth day:

inside a woman
ratty Kleenex, bread crumbs, tampons
deep clouds to shrink this mountain to a fleck of stone

oysters need irritants to fester a someday pearl

Sixty-seventh day:

trees groan to catch the moon, she
sieves her way through a mesh of branches
splashes the world
waiting below

Sixty-eighth day:

it takes more than what
we are, the sum of our parts
to see, takes our potential

Sixty-ninth day:

if you stand
still, enough
becomes a prayer

Seventieth day:

small lights are most welcomed
when one is lost

Seventy-first day:

rope is a tricky thing
along the trail snakes a green cord
diamonded with pink
to hang or to hold?
I wait
between dark trees

Seventy-second day:

this

       day is born

           between

              long

                  rakes

                      of

                          snow

                              and

wind

Seventy-third day:

the sound of creek under ridges and scars of ice
hollow murmuring
there is fire in water
muscled water
moving
we see only the surface of things

Seventy-fourth day:

love makes a good gravy — mix with flour, onions and a blind fork

Seventy-fifth day:

there are hallways and there are tunnels
it depends how
the light travels

Seventy-sixth day:

hands are laid on me today
and I am stronger for it

Seventy-seventh day:

the land reacts to our presence when we belong

Seventy-eighth day:

so much is revealed
after the leaves fall

Seventy-ninth day:

moon face veiled in red ash
hear coyote song carry the world
for a little while, prayers unravel
long threads of concentration connect
dark spaces

Eightieth day:

I walked a long time but I did not see miracles
unless you count this bag of blood and bones, placing
one foot in front of the other
and breathing

Magpie's whistle, flash
of white feathers on black

every day is sacred, every day a gift, understand

Eighty-first day:

courage is a shadow
she comes when the sun is low and makes you bigger

Eighty-second day:

rest here, inside Wolf's howl bag
in the blue of his throat

Wolf dances for Deer
between them, a black stone
heart gift from those who guide

Eighty-third day:

Crow, Raven, Owl of night
tell me what I've done is right

from a great height Crow coos
I shade my eyes, twist
back to see this ebony sliver
acerbic acrobat

Eighty-fourth day:

head	onion (several)
tongue	lightly salted water
heart	dusting of allspice
salt	pepper

Clean and scrape head with sharp guilt. Remove
eyeballs, ears and nose. Wash
thoroughly with common sense, saw
into pieces. Soak overnight in salt water. Rinse.
Place pieces in heavy regret size roaster. Add
water, to cover most mistakes. Simmer in oven
until meat is very tender and leaves of its own accord.

Eighty-fifth day:

my sister wondering where to go
when love is over
it is a death, resist the temptation to replay
every part
get to the dead part

close his eyes wrap him in prayers, light
a simple white candle
step over it
take a sweater from the hook and go

Eighty-sixth day:

if people wore mirrors
what would I see?

Eighty-seventh day:

steep hillside roots this tree
the more steep the hill
the straighter this one grows
arms outstretched to embrace the falling

such grace absorbs weakness
grows strong from it

Eighty-eighth day:

a trail is born
if it is taken

Eighty-ninth day:

rush sucks hard on my bones
turn open mouth to the wind
howling as lonely space can

my sisters lift their hands from tasks
turn heads narrow eyes sniff the wind
they rise
fill me with common sense soup
recipes for the sneezing root
take my cold feet in their warm hands

who needs a fucking hero?
sisters patch my bones with necessary needle sharp laughter
and the long broad thread of love

Ninetieth day:

small truths are the rules we should live by

Ninety-first day:

teacher, trickster are both message
and messenger

Ninety-second day:

if you don't say goodbye
can it be the end?
spirit, being thus, means
I will see you again

Ninety-third day:

as from the moon
there is no hesitation
Raven arrives on the fence

Ninety-fourth day:

the pause between friends
is the Creator taking a breath

Ninety-fifth day:

you are alone
that's all there ever is

taste cold dark water, the promise of snow
breath plumes white, walk
along slick, packed ruts, walk even
when the mountain is slippery

Ninety-sixth day:

back bone of the trail beneath my feet
stone faces find their smile between my fingers
Crow is here so
mostly
we are responsible for miracles

do your job
create

Ninety-seventh day:

on the trail, two deer
one nuzzling the other about the face
taking care of the other

as I sleep one hand creeps across to protect the broken one

Ninety-eighth day:

axe bites wood
wind snarls and grunts between the silent trees
make yourself ready
the weather is going to change

Ninety-ninth day:

shards and flicks of snow
pair of frantic eyes squeal, "Help! I'm drowning!"
those same eyes I once drowned in

because of the (s)now
I wave from the shore

One hundredth day:

my son ransoms this day
with three blue marbles he found in the alley
calm blankets my shoulders
flows water warm as blood
my son is the peace of a good, small room

One hundred-first day:

sage, sweet grass, lemon grass, bees wax candle, bergamot,
pink stone, inuksuk, mink, rough blue walls, iridescent
stones, antlers, hooves, dried pansies and a hummingbird,
peacock feather mask, crow feathers sewn with red thread,
raven and eagle and owl wings in a turtle bowl ringed gold,
words and worlds mapped by hand, arbutus chest plate, stone
maps from Saskatoon, Spain, New Zealand, Oman, Eire,
Brazil, spruce heart, birch bark box, moose hide, amber, egg
shells on a red background, the northern lights
pray this over and over again

One hundred-second day:

for those who mutter in their sleep
turn over and grab all the blankets you want
sleep this deep winter

use rhodochrosite to relieve stress

let it be, that I do
not age fifty years in one day

One hundred-third day:

among stones
small bones of the baby
scattered brittle, broken
hooves and hide of the mother
stilled on the bank of the river
dusted with dancing whorl of wolf prints

One hundred-fourth day:

the Methuselah tree
a bristlecone pine dignified by 5 000 years of life
her secret?
acceptance
grow slowly

One hundred-fifth day:

I came to photograph the tree
to have vivid memory of pine
for my eye when my hands cannot touch
found clean bird bone to fix my wrist

dream the protocol of preparation, leave stones
for the eight directions, a pinch of tobacco
for each
grandmother, grandfather, the Creator
and for me
bind the bone to my own

One hundred-sixth day:

the heart must be broken
to accept big love

One hundred-seventh day:

the temperature is -26C
sticks for the box I am making
clack in my ear, throat
on my tongue

snow shushes white through grass, through
gaps in the wooden fence, branches
stripped of raspberries, gooseberries and lilacs

across the valley
loons, trains and small planes leave us
ravens mimicking sticks clacking on frozen earth

One hundred-eighth day:

cold ground shrinks from stones
here now, threshold
have courage
then step

One hundred-ninth day:

tonight the Geminids peak
meteors fling themselves
from behind the curtain
northern lights rustle and chatter

spectacular events miracle the snow

One hundred-tenth day:

move past snow's sibilance
pay attention to avalanche growl

lead with the left shoulder
face the carnivorous north east wind
always
face the storm and walk

One hundred-eleventh day:

find a length of cold paper
let snow tick
take the crayon called mauve
start with that and do a sky
fog the orange crayon and pink along the edges
take the crayon called smoke grey
make the mountain chain stretch

if anyone starts talking stop right away

if it is still quiet
take your coyote crayon, release
a chorus just off the paper
under the crescent moon that only coyotes see

call this Tuesday
sign your name in crow

One hundred-twelfth day:

day knocks against the skin house
begs warmth begs light
through this sharp moon time
because of this dry cold time
my hair is blue with static
and my nose bleeds when fisted by frozen air

One hundred-thirteenth day:

memories permit
us to speak on things our heart
tends to in the night

One hundred-fourteenth day:

snow crunches and squeaks
the same sound that particular
stars or frozen dog turds make, after all
today is a working day
no time for chocolate thoughts

One hundred-fifteenth day:

self-respect differs from self-esteem
one bloodies your hands
the other is blunted by touch

One hundred-sixteenth day:

if you are still
pushing against the wall when
it falls, so will you

One hundred-seventeenth day:

to closely step in the tracks of another
makes the path easier
but less your own

One hundred-eighteenth day:

the tree sees this

unburden yourself to go far

One hundred-nineteenth day:

all this coyote scat on the trail
had led me as one blind

this week, I follow easily
reading what he leaves behind

One hundred-twentieth day:

ground sleeps
water does not
comes as cloud
creeps along arms of the mountains
covers us all quietly and completely

One hundred twenty-first day:

When I pack up my things and go,
who will stud my eyes with stars?
Who will scarf my hair with clouds?
Who will sing me to the stones?
Whose memories will rainbow my passing?

I will be snow, the raspy
cough of crows, wind
from the eight directions and the day moon
in her honeymoon slip. Who will know me?

One hundred twenty-second day:

the moon fills herself
one day at a time, becomes
solid
slowly

do the same

One hundred twenty-third day:

the Creator's hand opens
reveals Medicine Lake all stone and still
grey water, trees filled with May snow and first leaf
raw brilliance in a blue edged bowl

Hummingbird travels
through steam rising from the trail

One hundred twenty-fourth day:

be quiet
as a branch on the ground
placed there by unseen hands

One hundred twenty-fifth day:

eyes suddenly wide he lands on his ass rush of breath out
oof
aah inngh
scrabbles to find purchase
on the ice in the trail on the hill
off the edge
slides
shh
scratches
thin air
shh
stops
is still
still
still
by flick by flake
thick snow falling
red snow blooms beneath him

One hundred twenty-sixth day:

find one joyous thing to salvage
this day triage phone calls from Mom telling me that Dad's
lung collapsed
from friend turned stranger
from sister, stone faced as she rips her husband's favourite
shirt

a deer bounds into the trees just ahead
white tail blinking in the snow

One hundred twenty-seventh day:

every spirit sings when stroked
in turn, wind is both
fingers and song today
she touches everywhere at once
brings singing from my throat

One hundred twenty-eighth day:

my heavy tread
is the stomp of a child uncertain
burdened by questions

patience today
touch me with patience that I may deserve
the answers laid before me

One hundred twenty-ninth day:

face the sun
bless the wind to fill me
accept that all will right itself
it needs no push from me

One hundred thirtieth day:

putting my heart next to bark
invokes magic
not complicated upside down incantations passed
hand to hand from backs of nightmares, just
Raven
flies across cloudless sky
dips his wing to me

plumbing the distance between us
and finding it not too deep

One hundred thirty-first day:

sparrows fly from the Creator's book as pepper
as commas want, in a sentence
stretched to hold all, and everything,
the joy, being heard
sends Magpie into brilliant exclamation
everywhere, everywhere!
there is hope

One hundred thirty-second day:

leaves have stomata that open and close
to music, Vivaldi, cellos, big skin
drums, wind and water on stones
all occasion leaf to sing

One hundred thirty-third day:

How to harvest joy —

direct seed as soon as soil can be worked. Repeat
at two week intervals until late spring. Sow again in
late summer and fall. In harsh climate make
successive sowing all winter. Can be planted
in rows or sprinkled over a large area.
Joy requires light to germinate. Water
regularly; tears are fine, blood works on occasion.
One of the good things in life, almost
a balanced diet in itself.

One hundred thirty-fourth day:

do not forget who you are
every scar a flag woven from battle
wrinkled maps have their story

today, another story
will shakily right herself and walk

One hundred thirty-fifth day:

there is the song of a sea
in the tops of trees
in the grass
through the feathers of those who slowly watch me
walk across hills through mud

sky warms
the song of a sea, embraces the tops of trees

One hundred thirty-sixth day:

this day is between breaths
not so much held
as hopeful

One hundred thirty-seventh day:

speak as trees
slowly
and with full meaning

One hundred thirty-eighth day:

no more
dragging the body down muddied back alley memory
lane laced
with barbed wire leave the past intact

remnants
not remains

One hundred thirty-ninth day:

standing between storms
is a stone in the shape of a heart
a little broken near the edges
a little cracked here and there
glistening

One hundred fortieth day:

when you breathe
think on this
you are the candle lit
a heart as big as the sun
beating ancient rhythm

One hundred forty-first day:

the world is wrought by thought
make my words less and mean more

One hundred forty-second day:

this day is born
between two spring rituals
eating a salad to wake the blood
green onions, red tomatoes, celery, raspberry
vinegar and olive oil
after shoveling the sidewalk and wishing
there was roast chicken instead

One hundred forty-third day:

Cough Medicine —

1 onion chopped fine
2 tbsp. brown sugar
Melt enough honey to cover the onion. Mix
together, leave overnight.
Take 1 tbsp. at a time.

One hundred forty-fourth day:

this day is born in the first crocus
courageous outrageous flower
furred to brave snow streaked land
begins purple turns blue to
white pulsing
yellow centre
resuscitates bone hard heart of winter

good medicine survives

One hundred forty-fifth day:

in the soul
a clear cold time
tempers liquid

leaves bright courage

One hundred forty-sixth day:

working this piece dries my hands
the wayward shard of a river tossed elk skull
festers deep in the fatty part of my thumb
turns my silver rings black

the pelvis laced with antler tine
balances a wind chime of white bones
clunking sound muted by moss and lichens
my blood
spots red dries brown
is passed over by wind

this is good to know
all we pull together
will be passed over by Blind Eye Wind
and then
will not be

One hundred forty-seventh day:

if a stone presents itself to you
it is in trust
you promise to listen
repeat the song
as echo
as shadow
as long as necessary
you polish the stone
hold it up for Crow

if Crow coos to you
folds wings close to her black
self and twists in mid-air, it is written

One hundred forty-eighth day:

queen of her domain
the ruffled grouse strolls
along the fallen tree trunk camouflaged
when she descends to leaf litter feathered legs and all
it is an angel touching earth

One hundred forty-ninth day:

I walk with guardian
Badger, the aggressive healer needs
the sound of ice made water

thank you Creator for the stones lifted to my eyes
and the medicine left at my feet

One hundred fiftieth day:

shadow and light play on the path
listen, a door opens
light fingers flex themselves gently
mix the dark
muddled shadows run backwards, wary
mindful that without an object to attach to
light becomes love

One hundred fifty-first day:

Marten appears white face
mind blown wide opened we hear each other
his chidings are small chains churred against each other

head weaves from side to side
he moves to the next tree
two three steps up and chains stir again
more?
move?
he motions with his head the ground between us
bird hard eyes fix on me

he makes for the tree on the right then
down again
stops full face on me
the space between us wavers as through water
he melts
into the undergrowth of a forest suddenly so big

One hundred fifty-second day:

the sun warms the aphid to life
small pale green flames light the ends of aspen twigs

One hundred fifty-third day:

the Creator's ear is earth as we do not see it
make joyous noise if you want to be heard
get yourself a song and string from bone to bone
a home of light and wind

One hundred fifty-fourth day:

the creek is clear and cold
laughing her wet face along the stones
I stop, plunge aching wrist
wash me and mine

at first I thought it was because I would not let go
then know, no
it is after the weight lifts
that we feel her heaviness
the absence of weight can be disconcerting
all this is the letting go

One hundred fifty-fifth day:

our tracks take
from where we step

One hundred fifty-sixth day:

fir cones, rocks roll under foot
stick their tongues out at me
mischievous roots limp my ankles
scrape knuckles, elbow, hard cold shoulder wind
exhausted, I stop and look up
Raven chuckles and moves his sky

One hundred fifty-seventh day:

against any sky
smoke does not look like cloud

One hundred fifty-eighth day:

if we had eyes the size of fish scales
we could see beyond
the bottom line, rape, gutted boreal
land, corpse, oil sands
development would be eclipsed
by how happy the hairdresser was
when I gave him rhinestone earrings to match his bracelet
sparkly green and blue fish
scales in the sun

One hundred fifty-ninth day:

curiosity causes
cracks are fertile ground for
life, mocks any attempt to keep the surface smooth

One hundred sixtieth day:

this alpine terrain grey onion paper thin as ash
feet must be soft to avoid tiny delicate lace
like flower, moss, fungi, spider webs
be mindful

tobacco floats high in the circle and within my bones
breathes fire, earth
water and air

One hundred sixty-first day:

chivalry

carefully lift from the ground discarded calypso orchids
cradle an outsider's fit of remorse

four gentle eyed deer
lips quivering with sweet spring grass
let me pass

One hundred sixty-second day:

trees speak balsam fir
release fragrant tale of earth, of ash and sticky blood
fingers stroke the orange brown serge of bark
there is a giving
trees dance
from the earth's embrace
given the occasion

One hundred sixty-third day:

a-puff of dandelion
crouches under a fallen branch
a seed
child's wishing brush
strokes across the canvas of stones
suppose, floats the sky

One hundred sixty-fourth day:

one day's miracle is another day's river
the converse is also true

One hundred sixty-fifth day:

my son spied a feather as he biked to school earlier today
thunder clouds rumble, the wind picks up
he tells me to hurry if I want it

as I go
I send a message to someone who has forgotten me

feather catches me in the throat
an owl's feather, used to banish deception
so
silence too is a message

One hundred sixty-seventh day:

a hand fisted in anger
already holds all it can

One hundred sixty-eighth day:

courage

the stubborn streak that chains you to this dark place
will also see you win the race

One hundred sixty-ninth day:

flowers grow without
hand or hoe, stones
spring whole from the earth
sultry sage smokes time

on that hillside
along the top of that ridge
I walk there
and back weaving as deer do
for food, for a better view, crossing
rows of thought of time of light, I laugh
become smoke

One hundred seventieth day:

She said, "There is a cougar on the ridge
a raging cow elk in the creek."

half of me stayed home
the other half went looking
and found
thigh bone wrapped in fur as tight
as the gift I wrap for my husband's new office
long black stone bound in moose hide
the cougar has leadership medicine
and me
I am the raging cow fussing with scat

One hundred seventy-first day:

Magpie's back balances white blades of fear
and trouble, she pokes me hard
with black eyes

leaves me weightless

One hundred seventy-second day:

the heat of anger
does not warm (for long)

One hundred seventy-third day:

wolf willow and spruce gum
acrid, musky perfumes remake the world
a place where mended souls stir in the dust
turn over
and sleep
for another thousand years

One hundred seventy-fourth day:

the grizzly's paw print slowly fills with water
I look and realize
it should already be filled with water unless
the bear just moved, how
far is far enough? how fast?

One hundred seventy-fifth day:

today is a called the present
trees know this
their mouths filled to bursting with wind

One hundred seventy-sixth day:

my heart feels like a muscle again
for years you slippered around
wearing a merino wool sweater
vest the colour of hard rain
casually marking time
through the territory of my heart

today you are only a picture of you
my heart, no longer your place
feels like a muscle again

One hundred seventy-seventh day:

the Celts call these "thin places"
where the other side is so close the veil shivers your arms as
you reach through

the First People traveled these sacred pieces of earth
to think on things in the presence of the Creator

I know them as mountains
I see them with my spirit eyes
walk them with bone and blood legs

they teach
as clear bird song message, scolding squirrel lesson
bracing as clean water through moss

One hundred seventy-eighth day:

offer the peppery smell of leaves
small miracle that
doesn't compare with castles, museums or mosques
with cafés, operas or running the bulls in Pamplona

like that stone, there
I am content to be where I am

One hundred seventy-ninth day:

Ant smells a being, sucked to a shell by Spider
all feelers, legs then pincers
she takes the husk and carries it to
the end of the branch
drops it
because life is gone from it

One hundred eightieth day:

I watch
the deer looking at
the chipmunk
watching a dragonfly move toward
my husband who turns to me
watching the river
quiet as a burnished green blanket

everything moves as one turning

One hundred eighty-first day:

Ants foam over the tree
trying to target what I breathe on the bark
they move
on shiny point shoes, they click to the warmth
never doubting what they find will be useful

as my species too eagerly
seeks out heat or light never knowing,
if it will be for the loving or the learning
both, useful

One hundred eighty-second day:

Magpie sings this house to being
the world is made before I wake

still so far from me
the wisdom of black and white
approaches

One hundred eighty-third day:

find something big
to pit against, to throw loneliness into
shadow self safe
amid bone, snow and stone
moss, moth, hummingbird and me
the precious, the most tender, the delicate of design
we live here now

PAULETTE DUBÉ is the author of four books and the recipient of a number of awards. *Talon*, her first novel, made the shortlists for the 1999 Canadian Literary Awards, the Alberta Writers' Guild Best Novel Award (2003), and the Starburst Award (2003). Her poetry has garnered a number of rewards including the Milton Acorn Memorial People's Poetry Award (1994), the CBC Alberta Anthology (1998), and the CBC Literary Award (2005). *First Mountain* is a culmination of living in the mountains of Jasper for more than a decade.